Book publishing is a comparatively small but profitable and influential industry. Traditionally, it comprised many individual publishers, but gradually these have been bought by larger companies - the industry's 15,000 or so employees now work mostly for these bigger publishing houses, each of which comprises a number of smaller firms, known as 'imprints'.

Publishers still come in all shapes and sizes - there are plenty of small publishers which, like the larger houses' imprints, tend to specialise in a particular area - such as hardback fiction, paperbacks, children's books, education and so on.

Publishing combines creativity with commerciality, calling for people with good ideas, effective communication skills - and most importantly, the ability to survive a crisis and work to seemingly impossible deadlines!

The staffing of publishing houses varies - in small organisations, a job might include virtually everything, from commissioning authors to overseeing production and sweeping the floor! This booklet looks at the jobs connected with a larger publishing house and the processes involved, from the point when an author first thinks of writing a book ..... to the printed product on the bookshop shelf.

We concentrate here on what is known as 'Trade' publishing - mass market book publishing - but there are other spheres such as academic, educational and professional publishing, which cater for specific markets. Many of the processes involved in book publishing are similar to those in newspapers and magazines. For more information about them, read COIC's *Working In Journalism.*

ARROW BOOKS

This booklet looks at a variety jobs which are typical within the industry, using as its focus - Arrow Books. Andy McKillop, Publishing Director of Arrow Books, explains the history of the company:

'Arrow was the paperback imprint of Hutchinson, publishing middle brow books in the 1950s before it went downmarket in the '60s and '70s. In the mid '80s, Hutchinson was bought by Century and became Century Hutchinson. Arrow became its paperback imprint and began publishing the Century hardback list as well. In 1987, Century Hutchinson was bought by Random House.'

Arrow is now the mass market paperback imprint for all the hardback books published within the Group. In 1990, the Vintage list was launched, offering up-market literary works in paperback.

Edito
Depar

The editorial department is the cen
company. It's the editorial staff who make the initial decisions about
which books to publish. They are responsible for commissioning work,
for negotiating contracts and for making sure that the manuscript is
well-structured, grammatically perfect and, above all ...... going to sell
plenty of copies! Liaison with other departments is crucial. Sales
representatives, for instance, who deal constantly with the bookshops,
know whether a particular book is likely to sell to their clients in the
form suggested by the commissioning editor. The art department works
closely with editors to design the best jacket for the book. The
production department liaises over publication dates. And the publicity
department discusses interesting ways of marketing the product.

SECRETARY/ASSISTANT

The job of secretary/assistant is the first but all-important rung on the editorial ladder. It's a job that's not easy to find ..... competition is fierce as the market is swamped with eager graduates. And once you've found that elusive assistant job, the next steps up to assistant editor and thence to commissioning editor can be equally hard, since few jobs are advertised externally, so much depends on who you know.

ANDREA HENRY is an graduate with an honours degree in English. Even for her, it was hard to get a foot in the door:

'After I'd graduated, I started buying Monday's media *Guardian*, where all the publishing and media jobs are advertised. I sent off around eight applications each week as well as plenty of speculative letters asking whether people could give

me work. I wrote for all kinds of jobs - in publishing, TV, magazines ..... even basic administration posts, but there are hundreds of applicants for every job so I had little response. I even taught myself to touch type to offer an extra skill. It was very demoralising; you think that, as a graduate, you'll be able to get a job at a reasonable level, but it just isn't so. Eventually, I wrote a speculative letter to the personnel manager at Random House. She asked to meet me and told me that she was getting 50 of these letters a week! I didn't get a job but was kept on her books. Eventually, I asked if I could come and work free of charge, just to get the experience. I started on that basis at Jonathan Cape (part of Random House) and it was while I was there that I saw my current job advertised internally. The people at Cape gave me a glowing reference and of course I was on

the spot (I just came down the stairs for the interview!).'

Andrea is secretary/assistant to commissioning editors Jo Frank and Elizabeth Buchan, providing secretarial support in the form of typing and admin' and making sure that deadlines are met:

'I get to read a manuscript if I want to (I can do that at home), which is a really enjoyable part of the job. If I found something really good, I'd tell Jo and if she agreed with my judgement, she'd follow it up. I co-ordinate the editorial processes; I arrange for manuscripts to be read by a freelance copy editor and type the 'blurb' to go on the back cover, which Jo writes. I give that to the art department to incorporate in their jacket design. The paperback blurb I write myself, based on Jo's hardback copy. At various stages, I proofread - jackets or covers and the manuscript itself (I proofread that at home and I'm paid for it as a freelancer).'

There's plenty of admin' in the job as well as answering enquiries. Members of the public may ring up to say they have particularly enjoyed a book and is there going to be a sequel? There may even be complaints to deal with. It's a varied and often hectic job, but frustrating if you're impatient to fulfil your editorial ambitions quickly. So what's the most interesting part for Andrea?

'I'm involved with so many different aspects of publishing, liaising with all the other departments - production, art, publicity and sales. You get to learn about the whole process. You learn about diplomacy pretty quickly too! The good thing about a job like this is that you're well placed to keep your eyes and ears open, waiting for the next step up!'

COMMISSIONING EDITOR/AUTHOR

There are two different methods of commissioning work for publishing. One involves the commissioning editor going out and looking for new work; the other involves agents sending in manuscripts. Most editors do both. There is also a big move towards 'vertical publishing' nowadays; the a publisher buys the 'volume rights' (both the hardback and the paperback rights) and, instead of selling off the paperback rights to another publisher, keeps them within the same umbrella company.

As Commissioning Editor and volume rights buyer, **ELIZABETH BUCHAN** buys books to publish in both hard cover and paperback. She buys in books (mostly fiction), to go on the Century list as hardbacks and then be published by Arrow as paperbacks.

Elizabeth is sent around five manuscripts a week by agents, but some well-known full-time editors have dozens. Unsolicited manuscripts, directly from aspiring authors, are consigned to an ever-increasing pile which will eventually be read by a reader who comes in periodically. Elizabeth has readers whose judgement she trusts and between them they look at most texts. Only a very small percentage of manuscripts sent in to editors ever get published. Some will be by established authors, others by new writers. Some well-known authors may feel stereotyped under their usual name and want to write under another. Certain texts may suggest the first of a series to the editor, who will then go back to the author and commission a sequel:

'If I pounce on one as being absolutely wonderful, I take it directly to the publishing director. If she agrees, I have to fill in all the necessary forms, detailing previous sales of that author in hardback and paperback, the size of the print run, the proportion likely to be bought by WH Smith, libraries, other countries and so forth, the amount promised in advance and the royalty to be paid. Then I work out how much revenue we're likely to get at that size of print run and whether that figure matches the advance. I'll phone or write to the agent and negotiate the clauses in the contract, agreeing the advance, royalty and territory - the countries where it may be published. It's finally polished up by our contracts department and everyone signs.'

'My next step is to work out a schedule for the book and give it an ISBN number which is used worldwide to identify it. An AI (Advance Information) form needs to be sent out to booksellers and libraries as well as our firm overseas, saying what the book is about and giving information about the print run and territories. The art department needs to be briefed so that they can design jackets. And I have to edit the actual manuscript, saying things like "I don't think this character works" or "You haven't got the tension quite right here". I have to be very tactful, though.'

After Elizabeth has O.K.ed the manuscript, it's sent to the copy editor and from them to the printer, who sends it back in proof form. This is corrected by a proofreader and returned to the printer who sends then it to Elizabeth as 'camera ready copy'. Once her department has checked it again, it's printed ..... and the book is ready to be sold.

Elizabeth combines running a home, a family and two careers ..... and still manages to appear sane! A degree in English and history led to her first career, in publishing. A lifelong ambition - to write - drove her to her second, as an author.

'I found it difficult to combine work and small children, but I found that I *could* write at home with them. I wrote three children's books (an adventure book, a collection of limericks and a book about Beatrix Potter), and then launched into my first adult novel, which was much easier to write. After all, we actually live in the adult world, so we can relate to it ..... the chasm between a child's perception and ours can be enormous.

'I'd already found myself an agent and she turned out to be marvellous ..... really worth the 10% commission! It's essential to have an agent. They know which editors may be interested in your book and exactly the right people to talk to, so they really offer a short cut. It's a bit like a marriage, though - you have to get on. That's why it's a good idea to meet several agents before you decide on one.'

Elizabeth's agent sent the manuscript to around ten publishers, telling them how good it was and saying that it was to be auctioned to the highest bidder on a certain date. Auctions can be pretty hair-raising. There's always the fear that no-one will turn up! However, the auction went well and Elizabeth was commissioned to write a second novel. Her third is currently being auctioned in America.

'I now write two days a week, from morning till night, which takes an iron will and endless determination, I start by writing a synopsis (a brief outline), chapter by chapter, and then constantly refine what I've written, writing and re-writing each novel about three times.'

How to find an Agent

Recommendation is always a good way to choose an agent. In the absence of any prior knowledge, you should ask around and check in the *Writers' and Artists' Yearbook*, published by A & C Black. It lists literary agents in the U.K., the U.S. and two dozen other countries. Each listing gives an indication of the sort of work they handle, the commission they charge and how to contact them.

The Association of Author's Agents is the trade association of British Agents. Members commit themselves to observing a code of practice in their business.

Their address is 79 St Martin's Lane, London WC2N 4AA.

COMMISSIONING EDITOR

JO FRANK **is the Commissioning Editor for Century, the hardback imprint, commissioning 'middle brow' fiction - mostly fiction by women, for women. She looks for new talent in the area of writing covered by people like Mary Wesley and Joanna Trollope.**

Jo's experiences offer some tips for would-be commissioning editors. A degree is more or less compulsory, but after that the competition is so intense that any extra relevant skill or experience helps. Everyone told Jo that she needed to be able to type for publishing work, so after her degree in English, she took a course in typing and signed on with a temping agency who specialised in jobs with the media and publishing. (There are several in London - they advertise in the media page of Monday's *Guardian*):

'I got a temporary job as production secretary in the production department at Conran Octopus who publish big coffee table books. I knew it wasn't the area I ultimately wanted to work in, but no job in publishing is purely secretarial - you're always involved in the activities of your department, so I knew it would be a good way to gain experience and get my foot in the door.'

Jo then religiously read *The Bookseller* and *Publishing News* weekly, where she found the job of secretarial assistant to the fiction editor at Sidgwick & Jackson.

Before she could go there, though, she had a phone call from Pan Books, where her CV had been passed on, and they took her on as secretarial assistant in the editorial department, working for the senior fiction editor:

'One of the things which had apparently made my CV stand out from other people's was the fact that I had had those two months' experience in production.'

It really does help to get any experience in publishing on your way to the job you really want. And be resourceful - offer your services free of charge if that's the only way in!

So what was Jo's next step?

'The woman who had first taken me on had moved to Century and after I'd been at Pan for two-and-a-half years, she rang me to offer me the job of assistant editor. That's the interim job between secretary/assistant and commissioning editor. My very first assignment involved being given a manuscript to edit and an author to look after - it really was in at the deep end.'

Career movement in publishing often happens through contacts like that. It's a good idea to get in somehow and then make contacts as you work. Jo explains:

'Depressingly few jobs above secretarial level are actually advertised.

The hardest career move to make is from secretary to editor. You either need contacts in another company or a gap to appear above you in the hierarchy.'

Jo was lucky. After only six months, her boss left and she took over the job. Her brief now is to find 'raw young talent' and work with them to build them into that middle brow area of fiction. So how does she spot this new talent? By reading avidly - talented young journalists, for instance, may not have contemplated writing a novel, but the quality of their work may leap off the page. Agents also send Jo work. Some may have just a kernel of talent which can be shaped and encouraged until it develops. Jo, the agent, and the author may spend hours discussing possible plots and developments and the author will go away and work on something new. Jo may feel that a new author is going to turn out to be something quite special - like Catrin Collier who wrote *Hearts of Gold*:

'I could see that it could be the start of a series, so I told the agent that I'd like to commission another immediately ..... I knew she was someone I wanted to keep on my books.'

Once contracts have been signed and the commissioning editor has made the initial suggestions to improve the text, the manuscript is passed to a copy editor.

FREELANCE DESK EDITOR

Freelance desk editors work on manuscripts (sometimes called typescripts), copy editing and later proofreading them when they have been 'set' into print. Copy editing involves making sure that the manuscript is well-structured, grammatically correct and accurate and consistent in detail - ensuring, for example, that if the action in a novel is set in a place called Middleton on page one, that the spelling doesn't suddenly change to Middle*tow* on page 230! Proofreading is the careful process of checking for errors like 'literals' - like '*the*' set as '*hte*' or chunks of text missing or repeated.

JOAN DEITCH is a freelance Desk Editor who works calmly and in isolation whilst everything bustles on around her. She says that you have to be a 'nit-picking Nosy Parker' to make a good desk editor, with enough concentration to focus your attention 100 per cent on the text ,so that no inaccuracy may slip through:

'I once edited a book where, when I worked it out, a pregnancy lasted 13 months ..... you really have to keep an eagle eye out for all the details! Authors get very weary writing and re-writing, and my job is to look after them, tidying everything up after they've finished. Every desk editor has their own routine. I go through slowly first and copy edit, changing any repetitions, cutting the text and making lists of spellings and dates to check throughout the book. If any queries do crop up, I jot them down to ask the author. That first reading is really to give me the feel of the book. I make notes for the jacket blurb I'll write, noting down any particularly good quotes.'

After the first read through, Joan has a rest to clear her mind before spending a couple of days reading it through as a member of the general public might read it - just enjoying it, with her feet up! She's likely to pick up numerous errors she's missed. The third stage involves sitting down at her word processor and typing a letter detailing any queries, which she sends to the author with the edited manuscript and copies to the commissioning editor. The author then carries out the changes before the text is sent to the production department, who mark it up for the typesetter. Several sets of 'proofs' are sent back from the typesetter and a fresh pair of eyes

proofreads. (Joan will do this for books she hasn't copy edited.)

'For proofreading, you have the original manuscript in front of you, together with the proofs and a red and a blue pen, using red for typesetters' errors and blue for others. It's a bit like driving and continually looking in the rear view mirror - you need to check the proof against the original every few seconds. There's a special set of marks for correcting proofs which you have to learn. You mark the text where the mistake occurs (like putting a comma instead of a full stop) and you put a corresponding mark in the margin. If the text has been carelessly edited in the first place, you can really be in trouble!'

Proofreading is a job which Joan finds balances well with her editing. The latter requires a critical mind, while proofreading 'gives the brain a rest', merely demanding accurate checking. Writing a jacket 'blurb', on the other hand, tests her own writing skills.

It's a job which Joan loves, giving her a fund of anecdotes. She has just finished editing Michael Caine's autobiography:

'His typing was very chaotic, so I had to read the words aloud to get the feel of the sentences. Twice I couldn't do so because I was laughing so much. I roared! And twice I stopped because I was so moved.'

The variety of Joan's work makes it fascinating and stimulating, ranging from *The Menabilly Letters*, involving Joan organising and editing an accumulation of 30 years' of Daphne du Maurier's letters to a friend ('a lovely book'); to proofreading the *Lovejoy* novels ('like flying through the air!')

Joan came to freelance work after she'd given up a job as an editorial assistant with WH Allen to bring up her children:

'I began reading books for a Book Club, helping them choose the titles for their list. I built up a good network of contacts - which is the basis of successful freelancing. When I left Allen's, they kept offering me editing, proofreading and blurb-writing work ..... and it's built up from there. If you're freelance, you have to be prepared to take on any work. You never dare say 'No', even though it may lead to some pretty hair-raising moments when you've over-committed yourself! At least I can work evenings and weekends if necessary - it's a very irregular life.

'If you love books, it's wonderful. And you find that you build up a special relationship with an author as you edit their books over the years. Commissioning editors tend to use the same copy editor for an author so that they have a consistent approach. They need to know an editor's work and trust them. We have to be totally reliable. You can't spread your net too wide in this job. It's better to become the right hand person to the chief editor in just one or two publishing companies.'

Joan recommends the Publishers' Association pamphlet, *Careers in Book Publishing* as an excellent source of information. The organisation Women In Publishing is a friendly, informal contact point for women who want to enter publishing or are already established in the profession.

Literary Agent

A literary agent can dash the hopes of an aspiring author ..... or nurture a latent talent so that it flourishes and produces a book to impress the literary world. Agents can open the door to fame and fortune ..... or even modest success, hitherto unattainable by a fresh new author. Their power is considerable and a good agent uses that influence to get the very best deal for an author - with the most appropriate publisher. Nor does the arrangement stop there. There may be possibilities for TV or radio adaptations, translation or merchandising opportunities. The agent will see to it all. They offer business management and advice - acting as part accountant, part lawyer, part mentor. Literary agencies abound in London and the south of England. Some agents prefer to be self-employed, often specialising in a particular subject or area of work.

CAROL SMITH is a highly regarded Literary Agent who works from her home off Kensington High Street. She is well-known for spotting and encouraging new talent - a predilection which may mean that she waits a long time before some of her clients earn her any money:

'I'm sent hundreds of manuscripts which I read avidly. Most I reject. A few are good. Some have a grain of talent which leads me to talk to the author and say, "Let's forget about this book, because I can't sell it. But let's talk about your next one". I'll agree to represent them and encourage them, though it could be years before we get a really big success. I'm only paid for what I sell, on a commission basis, so I could be working free of charge for quite some time! But it's worth it when the talent is so obviously there.'

The agent's role is to represent the author's best interests, finding the right publisher, looking after all the financial aspects of their work, negotiating deals, sifting through contracts with a fine tooth comb, chasing up bad debts and keeping an eye on the publisher's publicity to make sure that the author is being promoted successfully. On publication day, Carol goes around the bookshops, making sure that displays are sufficient and successful - and if they're not, she rings the publisher to say so.

'When I sell a book, I see to all the legal aspects and the negotiating, keeping the author's accounts and gathering in the money so that all the author has to do is write. I deal with newspapers, magazines, TV, film companies and the publishers, making sure that all possibilities are exploited and that I get a better deal than the author would be able to get for themselves. It's important to retain as many rights as possible. The publisher may buy the UK rights but the author needs to retain American rights, film rights, merchandising rights and so on.'

Agents have to be alert to what's going on around them. When there are opportunities to be seized, Carol will spot them. A cookery writer's book may be helped by a promotion for the Egg Marketing Board or the endorsement of a new kitchen gadget; an artist or cartoonist's work could offer the chance of some merchandising, not only adorning products such as mugs, oven gloves and T-shirts, but also made into jigsaw puzzles, board games, CD and video games. Once a client is successful, deals like these can even be agreed before the next book is written.

Carol will know if a photo opportunity is unwise or which TV commercial could pay off. Anything not handled by the publishing company will be taken care of by a good agent. She will also know whether a book would adapt well to film, TV or radio ..... and then she'll negotiate the best terms:

'It's my job to keep an eye on how a

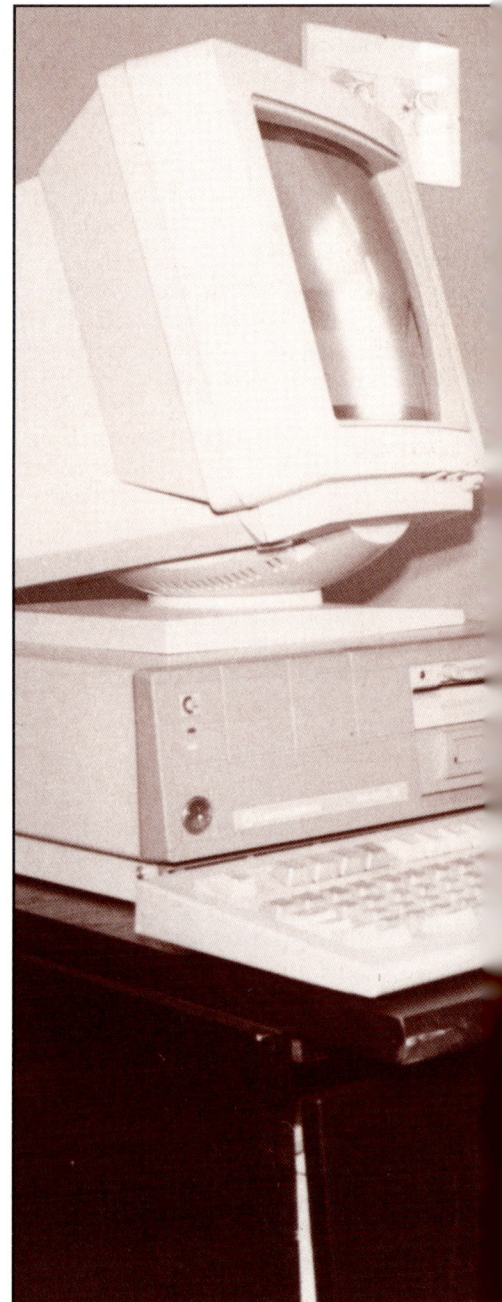

book is selling and whether a publisher is keeping it in print. If things aren't going as well as they might, I will negotiate to move the author to another publisher, who will buy the rights to previous books as they go out of print. That's why you may suddenly see a book by an author you'd forgotten about, in a brand new jacket and a bright new display - it simply means that another publisher has bought the rights and has issued it afresh.'

Carol has 60 people on her books but agencies will have many more, usually with individual agents specialising in distinct areas such as negotiating contracts or dealing with TV companies. Carol prefers the continuity of seeing the whole process through from start to finish:

'I'm interested in the actual writing of the product. The client and I will work together at great length to develop and refine their work. I may feel that someone who has written a novel would be better suited writing for TV and I'll encourage them in that direction. Someone with a wonderful ear for dialogue may be best suited to radio plays. It takes time and thought and commitment. It's a 24 hour day, seven day a week job ..... and I love it!'

So how do you become an agent?

Carol worked as a secretary in publishing companies on both sides of the Atlantic, seeing how the wheels grind and learning the jargon. From there she made the decision to become an agent and joined an agency. The progression to self-employment seemed a natural one. She recommends a grounding in the field which most interests you, be it publishing, TV or film - at any level, however menial.

Literary agencies and agents are listed in the Writers' and Artists' Yearbook or may be contacted through the Association of Authors' Agents. (The address is at the end of this booklet.)

Art Department

The art department's work can be what sells a book, particularly a paperback. Faced with shelf upon shelf of equally unkown paperbacks, how else may a buyer choose which to reach for, other than by the appeal of the cover? Having picked it up, they may turn it over to read the blurb on the back. They may even flick through it. But that first step in making a choice has already been taken.

ART DIRECTOR

SARAH PEARSON is Art Director for Arrow, Century and Red Fox children's books:

'We get involved after a title has been bought and given a publication date. The editorial department gives a 'presentation', telling us about the book, its author and their track record. We all discuss how we want it to look. It's possible to push a book in a certain direction by altering the cover design only slightly. For instance, if a woman's romance is set in the post-war countryside, we may decide to echo that period very definitely in the cover, to attract a certain reader. If we catch the right market, we increase sales on that and future books by the author.'

To get it wrong could be disastrous. If silver foil letters scrolled across a novel by a modern-day Virginia Woolf, the buyers it attracted would be sadly disappointed in the content! It's vital to get it just right, aiming at exactly the sector of society that would most appreciate the book. Bookshops arrange their books according to category and may themselves be influenced by the cover as they set out their stock. If a book is in the wrong section because of a misapprehension, thousands of sales could be lost.

Unless it's a sequel in a series she knows, Sarah reads most of every manuscript she deals with, making sure that she's grasped the essence of each book:

'We have internal department meetings to discuss ideas, approaches and possible artists or photographers who could be commissioned to produce a suitable cover. Artists and photographers all have their own style - you wouldn't commission some keen on vibrant surrealism to produce a pretty cover of a rural scene.'

Sarah has two full-time designers in her department, with one part-time consultant. She also uses freelancers if the department's especially busy or if the

designer has a particular skill. All artists and photographers used are freelancers - the art department's role is to design the look of the cover, arranging the commissioned artwork or photograph together with the necessary typescript or lettering to produce the most effective result:

'You can really build up a strong identity for an author, which readers will recognise and respond to when they buy. We spend a lot of time, effort and anguish in producing the end result. We have to capture the feel of the book and present it in a way which will most appeal to the audience we believe will enjoy it. Sometimes we have an exact idea which we can write down, or we may sketch a suggestion and find photographs of scenes or models in magazines and send them off to the artist.'

Sarah chooses her artists from glossy books of artists' work, sent to her by agents:

'When artists are successful, they get themselves an agent. It's expensive for artists to get their work in an agent's

book, but it pays off because we can be reasonably sure that they are experienced artists who know how to handle a commission and have the commonsense to work to a brief, keep to deadlines ..... and not throw a tantrum if their work's sent back for changes! We're always inundated each autumn, though, with recent art school graduates who want to come and show us their folders. Those who really persevere get to see me eventually!'

The chosen artist is sent a manuscript and a brief, suggesting an approach. They send back a rough pencil sketch of their ideas and it's discussed within the art department and with the editor and the sales department. There may be two, three or even more roughs before everyone is happy that it's exactly right. Once the artist has sent in the finished piece of work, the designers in Sarah's department start to add the type.

FREELANCE DESIGNER

Freelance designer **JANET WATSON** takes up the story:

'The editorial department give us the cover copy and we 'set' it, either using the Desk Top Publishing (DTP) programme on our Apple Mac computer or sending it out to typesetters. We may also commission special hand lettering. The editor proof reads the result and then we send our disk off to the typesetter to provide a bromide of the type, making it into camera ready artwork. We then make a colour visual, combining the type and illustration, so the other departments can see what the cover will look like before it's finally printed.'

These visuals are presented monthly at a meeting with the sales and editorial departments, where final 'fine tuning' may be suggested. Then the covers are ready to go to the printer. Printer's proofs are checked for colour quality against the original transparency. Occasionally, even at this stage, a cover may need to be redone. When sales reps take their advance covers to booksellers, they may be told that, given a different cover, they would definitely buy it. If this reaction is the norm, work must begin all over again.

Janet works 'in-house', mainly on Red Fox children's titles:

'These might be completely new books, or Sarah gives me the hardback book and asks me to produce a cover for a paperback version. Some covers stay the same, but others need jazzing up. Paperbacks have a more mass market audience, so the cover has to be more attention- grabbing on the shelf, readily appealing to the buyer. For some publishers I commission artists and photographers, but here I deal only with type.'

The job has changed enormously since Janet first qualified from a 'design for printing' course in Glasgow. One of the skills she learned was hand-lettering but now, more and more things are designed on the computer. Janet is still adamant about the value of a thorough training:

'There are all sorts of finer points about typography and design that you learn at college - letter spacing, position of type and the colours used all go to achieve the perfect balance. So much is lost if people just bash something out on their DTP programme ..... and if something goes wrong with the computer and you haven't got the traditional skills, you're sunk! The computer is an excellent creative and time-saving tool when it's combined with good design and training.'

Janet's work as a freelancer is extremely varied. Her specialities are children's books and non-fiction, art, crafts and pottery titles. Work comes largely through the contacts she built up when she first went into publishing and subsequently as her network has expanded:

'I design the inside of a lot of school books for the National Curriculum. I become an expert on a subject for a couple of months and then forget it all when I become involved in the next project!'

To become a designer, you need an art school or design college training. After that, your first step towards a job is probably going to be the most difficult. Janet says she wrote to every publishing company and advertising agency in the 'phone book, asking for a job. It paid off ..... it landed her a job as assistant art editor in a small publishing house with an art department of two! From there she moved to London as General Books Designer with A&C Black who produce many craft and pottery titles. Sarah started at Arrow as a junior designer, a job she saw advertised in the newspaper, but she does emphasise that people do tend to start as a general dogsbody, pasting up artwork, wrapping parcels to send to artists and generally helping with design jobs. Gradually, you'll be given your own jobs to work on.

It's very difficult to go freelance straight from college - far better to have had a few years in the industry first.

So why go freelance at all? Janet saw that it would pay more and offered greater freedom and responsibility, although it carries the uncertainty which all freelancers have of not necessarily knowing where the next job will come from.

Freelancers can get involved in many areas - for instance, mass market paperbacks, hardback books, company reports, brochures or publicity. Each requires a different style of designing. Janet stresses the importance of a wide range of work in your portfolio. If you know the sort of publisher you would like to work for, construct your portfolio around their needs and target them specifically. And, says Janet, it helps to be at least vaguely interested in what you're designing!

The up-side of the job is that it offers tremendous variety with the excitement of watching a project evolve over the months. The down is that you have to be able to accept criticism. When things go wrong, you have to be able to take a deep breath and start all over again. You need an eye for detail ..... and you also need a sense of humour!

PICTURE RESEARCH

Picture researchers find suitable pictures to illustrate books. Some designers do their own picture research if any is needed. Full-time staff researchers are likely to be needed to find suitable cover photographs or inside plates for literary 'classics' or 'personality' books. Other picture researchers work freelance, accepting commissions and then scouring photographic libraries, government departments, press agencies, museums and galleries for the subjects they need. The picture researcher is also be responsible for clearing and copyright restrictions or negotiating fees, as well as for the eventual return of the picture to its owner.

Researchers tend to specialise in a particular field and may well have specialist knowledge of a specific subject - such as science and technology.

Jobs in picture research tend to be given to people who already have experience. Work in a picture library is a good way in. There is a directory which lists current members of the British Association of Picture Libraries and Agencies (BAPLA), available from the address at the back of this booklet.

The Book House Training Centre offers a two-day training course in picture research, offered as an evening course. Twice a year, the London School of Publishing offers an eight-week course with one lecture each week.

Production

The production department of a publishing company takes the process from the edited manuscript stage right through to the printed book. It's their responsibility to organise the typesetting, proof reading, paper purchasing, printing and binding of both the text and the cover. They must make sure that the book comes out on time, meeting the deadlines set a year or more in advance. And they must keep a rein on the costing of the book so that the whole of the production process falls within their specified budget.

GROUP PRODUCTION DIRECTOR

STEPHEN ESSON, Group Production Director of Random House and Production Director of Arrow, explains:

'At the beginning of the process, we allocate a budget to the book, agreeing how much it's going to cost to produce. That means deciding on paper weight and quality and on the eventual size of the publication. A lot of the books we handle are offsets, meaning that the Group's already produced them in hardback and we are now going to publish a paperback. We work out whether it can simply be reduced in size and reproduced for the smaller paperback or whether it has to be completely reset by the typesetters.

Technical problems like reducing photographs have to be solved as well.'

Changes in publication date affect the production department dramatically:

'There may be a major author tour - like Michael Caine planning to visit various venues - so the publicity department will ring us up and say 'Michael Caine's doing a publicity tour ..... can you make sure the book is ready two months earlier than we'd arranged?' All the stops have to come out then, hassling the people in-house as well as the printer. We carry the can if it's not out on time. The buck has to stop somewhere ..... and it's here!'

If a manuscript is late, the production department still has to meet the deadline. It's a pressurised job. If a paperback has sold well and has to be reprinted, the production department must turn it round as quickly as possible - paperbacks have a short shelf-life, so if you take too long to produce more, you've missed the boat because people will be buying a more recent bestseller.

Stephen Esson sees it as a challenge:

'At any one time, you have so many books at different stages of production. It's like the Chinese entertainment of spinning plates on sticks. You need to know at exactly which point you can leave one project to do a bit more on another so that everything doesn't collapse! Production people need a strong commercial streak - you're a buyer as well, haggling to get the very best price from paper producers, typesetters and printers. As a Group we spend £18 million a year on typesetting, printing, paper and so on - I have to be sure we're doing it right!'

PRODUCTION CONTROLLER

MANJIT SIHRA is a Production Controller, working directly to Stephen. After her degree in English and history, Manjit wasn't sure what she wanted to do so she took a job as a temp. That's when she decided on publishing:

'I was temping at Faber & Faber and I loved it. I got a job as editorial assistant at Futura and after eight months moved to Penguin as a secretary. Two years as production assistant with Collins followed that before I moved here as production controller.'

Manjit covers the Century fiction list and business books:

'I work from the typescript stage right through to the finished copies in the warehouse - organising typesetting, proofreading and printing. Things rarely run completely smoothly. There's great variety in the job, particularly when colour plates are involved and their quality has to be checked. (Especially important in the publishing of children's books, where there's a lot of colour and plenty of pictures.) Printers send 'running sheets' for us to check the colour and photographic quality - they are sheets purely of pictures and plates. After they're printed, folded and gathered, sheets are sent to us for checking before they're sewn and glued together.'

There's always a certain amount of chasing up to be done, politely hassling everyone to make sure that they finish their part of the job on time. It involves a lot of liaison with the publicity and sales departments over the proofs of jackets and covers. Artwork is sent to be proofed by the jacket or covers printer. (There's a different printer for the main body of the book.) Around 900 covers are printed in advance for the publicity and sales departments so that they can use them for publicity and showing to booksellers.

Manjit deals with all kinds of different people on the 'phone - with suppliers and printers, editorial and sales staff:

'You need to be diplomatic and able to keep the wheels oiled. There's a lot of responsibility and always some new crisis!'

Stephen Esson feels that the knowledge imparted through a degree course is not essential to do a job in a production department ..... but the competition to get into any job in publishing means that the majority of entrants do have a degree.

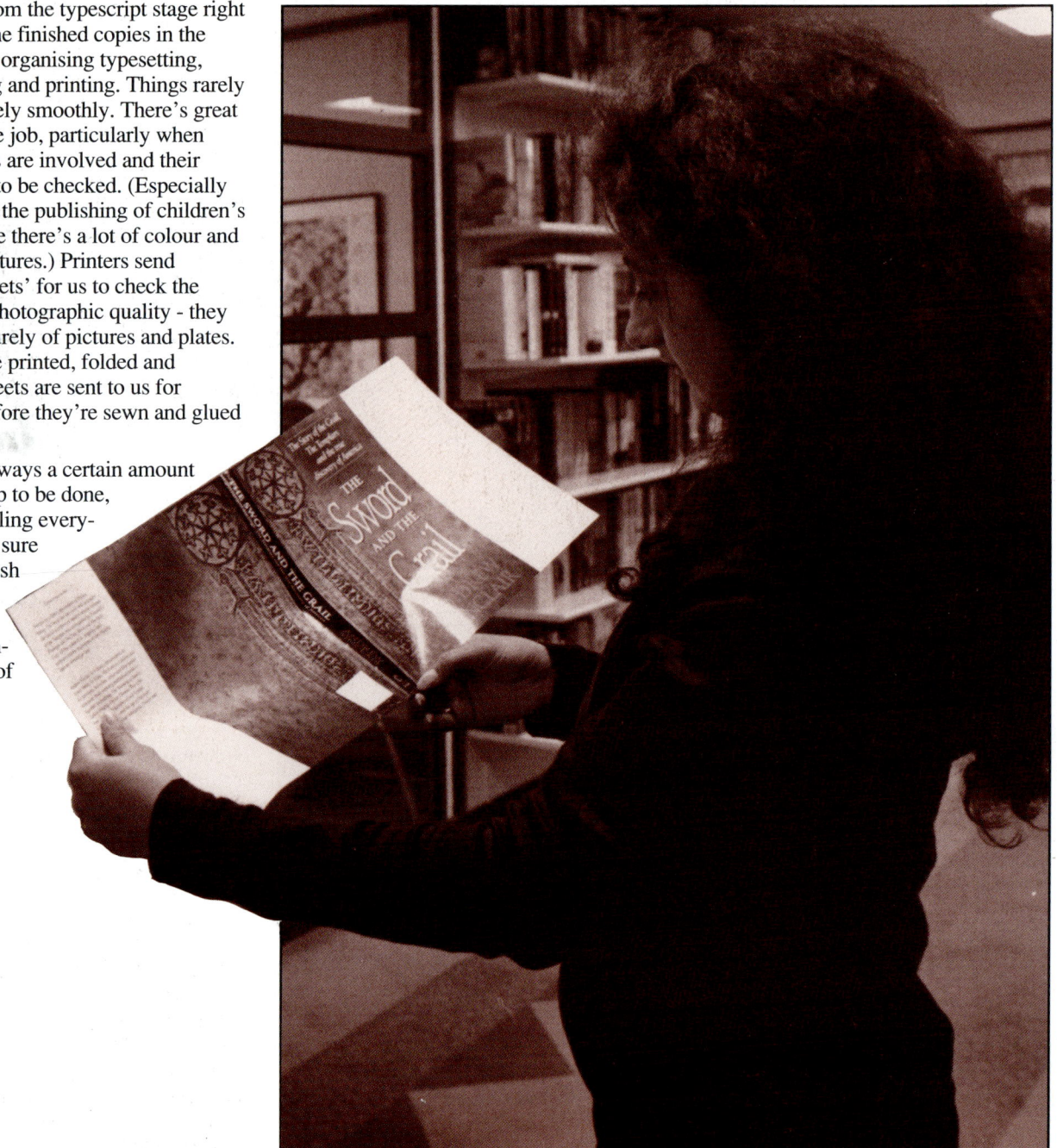

BOOK DESIGNER/TYPOGRAPHER

After a typescript has been edited, a typographer designs the layout, deciding how the inside of the book will look. That could mean marking up the manuscript so that when it's sent to the typesetter they know what instructions to type in; or, more probably nowadays, the typographer will be given the edited text on computer disk and use a Desk Top Publishing computer program to design and print out a layout to be used by the printer.

ROGER WALKER has his own design/ typography business:

'Not all books need the services of a typographer. If it's a straight forward novel, it will probably be sent directly to the typesetters with a copy of a book to use as an example of the sort of layout the publisher wants. That's obviously the most economical way for the publisher to do it. I'm called in when more of a design element is needed.

'That may be for a book which is all text but has complex chapter headings and subheadings, tables or footnotes to be designed - or it could be for an 'integrated' book which combines pictures and text. My job then is to decide exactly where the text and pictures are to go in relation to each other. The desk editor will give us guidance by, for example, telling us how many different sorts of heading there are. We interpret them visually so that they are consistent throughout the book.'

The typographer works out what the typographic specification has to be to make the book the right number of pages - that means choosing type size and font (shape) as well as elements such as different headings. Cost is a very important factor. Since the paper is a major cost in the production of the book, the aim is to lay out the book so that it's economical on paper but still pleasing to the eye. That's where the skill of the typographer comes in.

If the work is on disk, Roger does the page make up on screen using DTP, referring to the 'hard copy' (the typescript sent to him with the disc) as he goes along. He may spot the odd error that's been missed at a previous stage, in which case he'll let the editor know.

Photographs have to be 'scanned' in to spaces left for them in the text. Scanners are extremely expensive pieces of equipment and not normally kept by

typographers, so photographs for books designed by Roger are scanned in by a specialist 'origination house'. Roger is given all the photographs with the disk and hard copy and works out what size they will have to be to fit into the text. To show the publisher what the finished layout will look like, he pastes photocopies onto the layout he prints out

and sends to the publisher for approval. When his finished layout has been agreed, he sends the disk, a hard copy and the photographs to an origination house, leaving the appropriate instructions on size and positioning for the photos to be scanned in. The origination house outputs the whole thing on bromide or film for the printer.

Roger feels strongly that to get into typography, experience is more important than qualifications on paper, although he does point out that people come into the work at all levels.

The two main ways in are either via a training in graphics or through the printing industry.

You can take a graphics course at an art college, where you can specialise in typography; or you can take a degree in graphic communication, which includes training in modern technology.

Experience in the printing industry would be a useful way into typography, either working for a reprographic house or taking a printing course at college.

Graham Harmer, Roger's assistant, took a one-year course at the Berkshire College of Art - approved by the British Printing Industries Federation (BPIF). It covered design, printing and touch-typing and allowed him, immediately afterwards, to get his present job. The London College of Printing also runs courses.

Good GCSE/SCE passes in English, maths, a science and technical drawing are an advantage.

For details of courses, contact the colleges direct or the BPIF.

It's a good idea to try and get some work experience with a graphic design studio. Ask your school to make contact - or write to them yourself.

PAPER AND PRINT BUYER

finish will affect the printing. Paul Tasker:

'Grampian gives Random House the most suitable grade for each job, measured in terms of quality and value for money. We track each title as it's printed, liaising with the printer to make sure that the right specification of paper has been delivered and the correct amount has been used. The production schedules are updated every week, so that we know at any time the production stage every book is at. Stock control is also an important element of paper buying - we mustn't allow too much money to be tied up in stock, nor to have too little stock for the important reprints when they're needed.'

Paul has to keep an eye on a number of details. When a book is over a certain number of pages, for instance, he uses a lighter grade of paper: '1200 pages on standard paper would be like a brick!'

It's a specialised job, requiring a depth of knowledge not necessary in newspapers or magazines. The pulp which goes into making the paper may be mechanically or chemically produced - different pulps produce paper with different characteristics. The paper buyer must appreciate the implications and be prepared to compromise in some areas to achieve an objective in others. They spend a lot of their time talking to people - discussing problems with production staff, liaising with printers or talking over new developments with mills.

Paper and print buying are crucial to the quality of the finished book ..... and to balancing the production department's accounts! Some publishing companies use the same paper suppliers and the same printers each time; others use the services of a number of firms, negotiating new prices for each commission.

Companies may employ someone solely as paper buyer or print buyer; the print buyer may combine both functions; or the job of buying paper and printing services may fall to a member of the production staff.

Random House employs Grampian Paper to act as paper buyers on their behalf. **PAUL TASKER**, Grampian's Commercial Manager, explains the process:

'Paper merchants will have a number of paper mills on their books. They call on publishers and show them paper samples, recommending the most suitable of their range of products for each job. We are slightly different in that we aren't restricted to contractual agreements with a few mills ..... we can source from any suitable mill, so we can recommend the best material for any title, selecting from the whole spectrum of papers produced.'

Five per cent of the paper produced in the U.K. is used for books - and it's far from uniform. There's a tremendous variation in requirements. A merchant will show plain and printed paper samples in various weights and finishes from a number of mills. Each has a different appearance and will be best for a different purpose, bearing in mind the ultimate cost and estimated sales of the book. The higher the merchant's throughput (how much paper can be sold in a given time), the lower the price per tonne to the publisher. For example, if merchants can guarantee the mill a turnover of 2,000 tonnes a year, they will be able to buy the paper at a better price than if they had only a small throughput. And that cost can be reflected in the price charged to the publisher.

There has been a trend recently to publish larger extent (with more pages) books on newsprint because it is light and economical. Short extent paperbacks may use a heavier, thicker paper so that the end-product is bulkier and the readers feel they are getting value for money! Compare the books around you - there's an enormous difference between the paper used for glossy 'coffee table' books and that used for a mass market thriller.

Paper buyers need to know how each grade of paper is produced and how the

There are no specific requirements for a job in paper or print buying, except common sense and the ability to communicate well ..... and a knowledge of the processes is useful. Paul started as a general assistant with three A levels in maths, physics and economics, all of which are useful to his work. His technical experience was gained on the job, learning as he went along.

It is possible to take a degree in paper science at Manchester UMIST. For print buying, a qualification in printing is a distinct advantage.

There are around 150 paper stockist merchants in Britain - for further details, contact the National Association of Paper Merchants. (the address is at the back of this book.)

Typesetting

The typesetter's job is to transfer the words supplied by the publisher into a form suitable for printing. The advent of computerised systems has transformed typesetting - manuscripts are now keyed onto computer disk and stored on magnetic tape.
Publishers may do their own typesetting using a Desk Top Publishing (DTP) programme or, more usually, employ the services of a specialist firm who will advance the whole process for them.
Intype Input Typesetting Ltd. is an industrious firm of typesetters based in Wimbledon with a staff of 27. Each keyboard operator can average 100,000 keystrokes a day ..... that's a lot of typing!
Intype works for around 50 publishers, producing 80 books a month, ranging from slim paperbacks which have a production cycle for Intype of around three months, to hefty dictionaries which can take three years to complete. The firm also offers a service of book reproduction, photocopying books in advance of their publication for sales reps to use as 'sales proofs' - copies which they can take with them to show clients.

APPRENTICE TYPESETTER

JOANNA DRESCH has been an Apprentice Typesetter at Intype for three years and is nearing the end of her apprenticeship, soon to become a fully fledged 'Journeyman Printer'. Joanna's interest in graphics and experience in word processing (she had done a course at school) led to her job with Intype:

'When I first started, I was doing very basic work, learning the commands and how the whole system works. Gradually I was given further jobs to do, such as editing. I still find that I'm learning all the time. If I had a problem, there was always someone to help, so I never had to worry about making a mess of it.'

Joanna's apprenticeship combines practical experience with a three-year City and Guilds printing course which she attends for one day a week at college. The course is broader than her work at Intype, covering all aspects of printing, so she will have a chance to move into a different area of work if she wants to when she has qualified:

'I enjoy it. It broadens your horizons and you realise just how much there is to learn! So many different rules apply to each job - you have to concentrate and make sure that you're always accurate. At the end of the day you can be really tired, but when you eventually see the finished book, when you go into a shop and actually pick up your own work - it's really worth it.'

Joanna's job is to key in the text and codes, checking against the manuscript to make sure that the disk and manuscript match and that no pages are missing. When it's been proof read, she re-edits and paginates. She outputs it on bromide paper and it's re-read again in-house to make sure there are no mistakes before it is sent to the customer for a final check:

'It's a 9 - 5 job but there is the option of overtime. There can be a mad rush to get things done if the customer alters the schedule and suddenly wants things sooner. Then it's very pressurised. You can't hang about!'

You need to take a pride in your work to do Joanna's job - it has to be absolutely accurate:

'It's quite a responsibility. You know the book's going to be read by millions of people. I've done the odd bestseller such as a Dick Francis. It makes the job really interesting when it's a good book. But you have to be careful not to get carried away and read it!'

If you want a job like Joanna's, you need a good general education, with at least GCSEs/SCEs in English and maths. Training is on-the-job, with the opportunity to progress via day-release at college.

Publicity Department

The publicity machine starts moving way before a book is published. The rights to a new book may be bought three years ahead, before the book is even printed - for example, the rights of the new Salman Rushdie book, due out in 1995, were already tied up in 1992. The publicity department is made aware of future plans, but doesn't actually begin its work until nine months before the publication date, when they start publicising the book to the trade - the booksellers themselves - who need to know what's coming up around six months in advance so that their orders may be placed three months before the book appears. There are regular marketing meetings between the publicity, editorial, and sales departments to discuss plans. Nine months before a publication date, they talk about possibilities for a book's campaign. They will already have 'mock-ups' of the book's jacket, so they will know exactly how it will look. The exact market needs to be established and whether there is a special interest market that needs to be attracted. From then, the strategy will be fine-tuned and the campaign will begin.

PUBLICITY MANAGER

RACHEL CUGNONI is Publicity Manager for Vintage, an upmarket paperback imprint of Arrow Books, publishing middle to high brow literature. Rachel's first job was as a publicity assistant with a small publisher, writing 'blurbs' for book jackets, making show cards for display in book shop windows and arranging signing sessions with authors:

'It was such a small company that I didn't have a boss - I was the publicity department! I simply learned as I went along. I was there for one-and-a-half years, during which time I was actively looking for other jobs. I found one with Chatto & Windus, and moved from them to my present job. At Chatto I was responsible for producing the advertising posters - commissioning designers to design them, dealing with the printers - organising point-of-sale material, arranging promotional material, working out promotion budgets for books, thinking up marketing proposals and campaigns, buying advertising space in the media and writing advertising copy.'

People who work in publicity have to be endlessly inventive, thinking up new ways to promote books and writing copy that will make the reader want to buy that book rather than the one advertised next to it. For example, one of Rachel's colleagues organised the publicity for the new mass market 'sequel' *Wuthering Heights.* She and a friend dressed up as Cathy and Heathcliff and rode around London in a carriage to promote the book! Rachel is currently responsible for the new editions of Virginia Woolf, printed by Vintage as the author came out of copyright. Since the author is dead, with no new story about her to make for eyecatching publicity, Rachel had to identify another strong selling point ..... the fact that they are publishing the original, definitive texts first published by Virginia Woolf's own Hogarth Press, with appealingly evocative new packaging:

'I commissioned a beautiful poster to be displayed in bookshops which will catch people's attention and I mailed it to all the English literature lecturers at universities around the country, together with a complementary copy of the book. We also did 'giveaways' with the literary press - we sent them copies and followed up with a phone call telling them what Vintage were planning when Virginia Woolf came out of copyright. Then we got them to run a competition, the prize being a full set of all nine novels.'

In publicity, it's important to spot an opportunity and capitalise upon it. When A L Barker's *Element of Doubt* collection of ghost stories was due to be published in November, Rachel rang Radio 4's short story department and suggested they use it for a week of hallowe'en readings. In return we put 'As heard on Radio 4' stickers on the books. A publication date might even be changed if someone has a brilliant marketing idea around a book.

Rachel's approach differs according to the writer she's publicising. For John Pilger's recent *Distant Voices* she arranged readings by the author throughout the country in bookshops and art centres:

'The author reads from his new book, answers questions and then signs copies. Someone as well-known as John Pilger is likely to attract an audience of around 200 each time. I make sure each event is widely publicised, contacting radio, TV and the press. Even when an author is little- known and only a few people turn up, it's still worth while because those people tell their friends and also feel a special loyalty to the person with whom they spent an intimate hour. They're going to be more likely to buy current and future books.'

Rachel points out that half the battle is getting the bookshops to take the book on, so half of her promotional work is to the trade, the other half to the public. If she can persuade the bookshop to hold a booksigning, then the shop itself will be more likely to remember the author in future and so take more books.

There are two sides to book publicity - promotions (producing 'dump bins' and their 'headings' to display books in shops, organising posters and publicity) and public relations (PR), making sure that books and authors are publicised on radio, TV and the press. In some jobs people may specialise in just one area; Rachel is responsible for both aspects of the Vintage publicity:

'The hardback list offers a great P.R. opportunity because the titles are all new. The paperback list is made up of books which are essentially reprints of hardbacks, so there is less PR work and a greater emphasis on marketing the product in terms of advertising. We print 100 paperback titles a year, so that's a lot of publicity!'

Rachel admits that the job can be glamorous - organising dinners with authors and parties at the smartest clubs and restaurants, an expense account for endless entertaining. But she's at pains to point out that it's also hard work! To her falls the worry of whether the party will swing, whether a publicity stunt will pay off. A great deal hangs on the success or failure of Rachel's work. Contacts are essential to smooth the path and make her job easier. She has to be diplomatic, thick-skinned, enthusiastic and tireless ..... If you've got all those qualities, it could be for you!

A degree in English is essential if you want to progress further than secretary or personal assistant. Rachel knew that typing skills might be useful - but she was wary of becoming and staying a secretary. Consequently, she decided not to learn to type .... so there was no danger of being someone's secretary! However, she says that 80 per cent of the people on her post-graduate course entered publishing via the secretarial route.

Rachel's place on the London College of Printing's post-graduate diploma in Printing and Publishing was sponsored by Kodak. (Read COIC's *Sponsorships* for details of possible sponsors.) The addition of that course to her BA in English and history placed her a step above other publishing applicants and got her interviews.

Sales & Marketing

Sales and marketing staff are the front line of the publishing team. They are the people nearest the customer, who can find out what will sell and why. Their 'troubleshooters' are the sales representatives (reps) who visit booksellers to sell the publisher's wares. A back-up team furnishes them with new selling aids, useful statistics and fresh ideas to help win over the customer.

The sales department at Arrow is led by the Managing Director who deals with all the budgets and strategies for marketing the products. The Director of the Sales Team deals with the major 'accounts' (clients) such as W.H.Smith, giving presentations to explain and preview forthcoming titles; and the Key Accounts Manager deals with the smaller major accounts, mainly wholesalers, and is responsible for finding different ways of generating sales. The Sales Administration Manager deals with all the paperwork generated by the sales force, opening accounts for clients and organising credit terms. Her assistant makes sure that the stock ordered is in the warehouse on time.

It's the sales department that decides when a book should be reprinted and what the new cover price should be - a decision which must be quickly acted upon by the production department while the demand for the book is still there.

The outdoor sales force is made up of sales reps who have a list of bookshops to visit in their given region and call on them on a weekly basis, checking that they have enough stocks.

SALES SECRETARY

SOPHIE MEIER provides back up for the sales team, taking care of all their typing and dealing with enquiries. Sophie is also Secretary to the Managing Director and U.K. Sales Director of Arrow Books, running the sales office:

'It's a varied job. Sometimes I may be typing all morning, then assembling sales kits before rushing off to a marketing meeting. The pace varies from day to day.'

Sales kits are an important part of the reps' apparatus. Information on all titles for release in a particular month, is grouped together with information sheets which give details of any promotions being run.

The essence of the marketing side of the work is constantly to find new ideas, new ways of persuading people to buy books. It takes people who are innovative, imaginative and self-motivated. Sophie's own ambitions lie in marketing. She took a bi-lingual secretarial course with a marketing slant after her A levels and then 'temped' for a few months:

'I wanted to see what different office environments were like before I decided where I wanted to work. If you're a temp, agencies actually ask you whether you prefer an informal or a formal atmosphere - there are tremendous differences between one place and another. At some, you're expected to get coffee and remind your boss of meetings; at others it's far more informal and you're given more responsibility.'

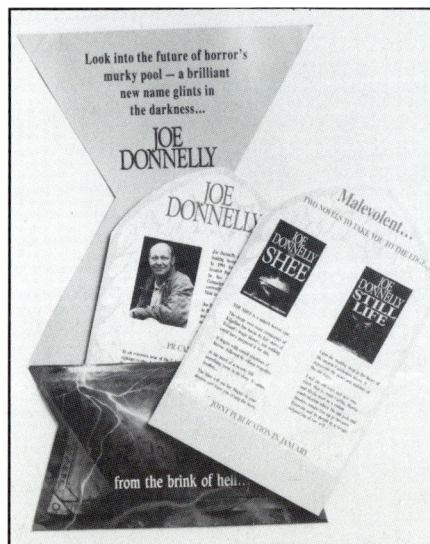

Sophie's first permanent job was with a small magazine publishing company, as secretary to the sales forces in the U.K. and abroad. After a year, she moved to her present job:

'This is a good way in because I have the opportunity to see jobs advertised internally when I'm ready to move on. It also gives me good experience. You have to have patience for my job - I may be in the middle of doing something very complicated, when a customer rings up and expects instant attention. There are constant demands from all sides but that's what makes the job stimulating and satisfying. It tests my ability to be organised, diplomatic and adaptable ..... but it's fun!'

To be a secretary, you obviously need to have secretarial qualifications. Remember, though, that if you eventually want to branch out from secretarial work you may have to be prepared to take further qualifications. Marketing/business studies qualifications are useful if your ambitions lie in that direction.

Look into the future of horror's murky pool — a brilliant new name glints in the darkness...

JOE
DONNELLY

JOE
DONNELLY

from the brink of hell...

SALES REPRESENTATIVE

DAVE WESTWOOD is one of Arrow's team of twelve regional Sales Representatives who visit bookshops throughout the country to sell the Arrow list. And it's no mean task ..... Dave himself covers the whole of the east of England from Newcastle right down to Lincoln:

'I have around 70 'accounts' to visit - fortnightly in the case of the bigger customers; monthly for most of the others.'

Dave gathers information about forthcoming titles on the Arrow list at the major six-monthly conferences at the head office, and the smaller two-monthly meetings where all reps are given details about new books, the authors and their track records. It's at meetings like these, with editors and the sales directors, that comments can be made on future cover designs and tips picked up on selling points:

'I always take a lot of notes - which I can look back at when I come to present the new titles to the accounts. I'll have been told things like how well the book did in hardback, if it made the bestseller list, whether it's being serialised on TV. I'll be able to judge how likely the cover is to sell the book ..... any major selling points that will make it stand out above the rest.'

Every month the reps are sent sales kits which include the covers of forthcoming titles (around thirty for presentation to bookshops each month), detailed information about each book and colourful 'presentation cards' which advertise the 'lead' titles - the books tipped to be the biggest sellers. Dave collates all the information in a presentation folder, together with any of the sales points he's picked up at previous meetings. He can also look back at the record card he keeps for each shop to see what they've bought in the past, using that information as back-up ammunition when he can! For instance, when presenting John Grisham's new novel, *A Time to Kill* to buyers, he can refer back to the author's last bestseller, *The Firm* and point out how well it sold. It's also useful to remember how well a book sold in hardback ...... *The Firm* was a flop in hardback, but it's success in paperback shows that buyers can't always tell from hardback sales if a book will go badly.

John needs to learn all these points before his first appointment with a new month's list ..... don't forget that buyers in bookshops are seeing reps from different publishers all the time. He has only a very short time to sell each title without risking 'buyer boredom'! It's his job to present the new list of titles in an interesting way, as succinctly as possible - buyers are busy people.

'There are three elements you can sell about a book - the author's reputation, the cover, or the storyline. You don't waste time dwelling on irrelevant points. The more often you call, the easier it is to sell - after all, you can divide a month's list in two and concentrate on half the titles if you call once a fortnight instead of once a month. That way, each title has more chance.'

Dave has a journey plan worked out on a four-weekly rota so that he knows at a glance which towns he's visiting on any one day. Within that timetable, he makes individual appointments with buyers, allowing time to check stock levels and note down any books the buyer wants to return (because they haven't sold). After 14 years with Arrow, he's got it down to a fine art:

'You build up good relationships with buyers over the years and develop a mutual trust. There's no point in smooth talking them into buying more than they can sell or a title that's not suitable for their market - it'll only mean that they don't trust you next time round.'

It certainly seems to pay off - Dave spent a whole afternoon in a bookshop in Newcastle recently, but he left having sold 1700 books!

There's a certain amount of paperwork linked with the job. Every day, Dave adds up all his orders and sends a weekly figure up to head office, together with an estimate of whether projected sales will match his target number of books to sell. Since he's not paid on commission, targets don't result in undue pressure. They're simply there as an indication of how many books should be printed. After all, if the key accounts manager and the reps between them take orders for 150,000 copies of one title, there's not much point in going ahead with a print run of only 100,000. Similarly, if it looks as though a book isn't going to sell as well as they thought it would, there's still time to reduce the number printed ..... reps sell the books to the shops about two months before they are actually printed.

So how do you become a rep? It's something of a Catch 22 situation because publishers like reps to have experience - but of course it's difficult to get experience if you can't get a job! Experience in any area of selling is an advantage; bookshops are a very good grounding.

Before going to an interview, it is a good idea to familiarise yourself with the publishers' books, as you will probably be asked what you know about the company.

To be a rep, you don't always need academic qualifications (that varies from one publisher to the next), but a knowledge and enthusiasm for books are an advantage. You're selling yourself to a certain extent, so you need to be smartly dressed and outgoing, able to put people at their ease and build up a rapport. As a trainee, you'd go out with a senior rep to see how the job works, gradually attempting it yourself before you're let loose on your own!

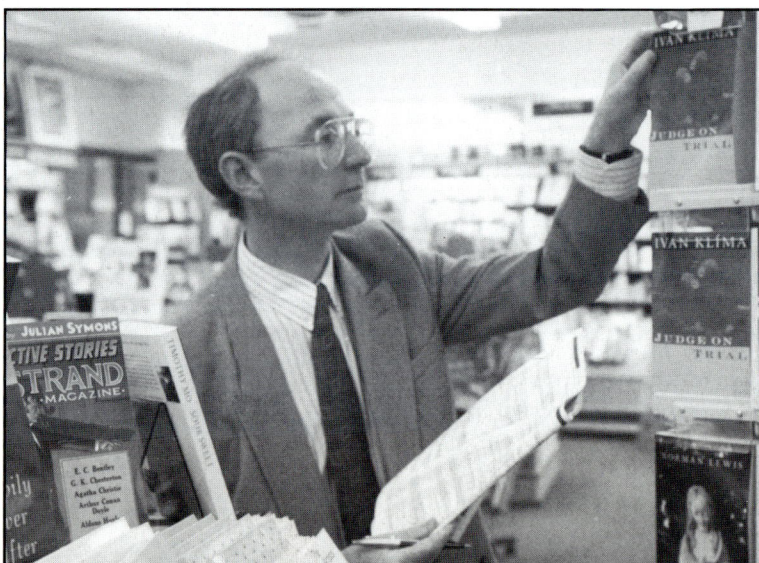

Desk Top Publishing

Desk top publishing is something of a misnomer because a desk top publishing computer program does the work not of the publisher, but of the specialists who prepare the text (whether books, newspapers or magazines) for printing.

A file of text from a word processor on computer disk can be transferred to a computer using a DTP program and it can then emerge in a state from which camera ready copy can be produced. All the processes can be carried out by just one person, with a DTP program. Text is given invisible 'tags' which refer to typeface style and size, word spacing and so forth. The program uses the information to format the text automatically, laying it out on the page in accordance with the instructions it has been given. The end result is a complete page layout which can be viewed on screen.

DTP is an increasingly important skill to learn in publishing nowadays. It is widely used, allowing designers like Sarah Pearson and her art department at Random House to design the cover of a book ..... and enabling typesetting firms such as Intype in Wimbledon to provide a speedy and accurate service to customers.

DTP programs are also used by people who want to set up their own publishing business - people like **KEN EDWARDS** whose full-time job is as a freelance journalist. Ken used to write poetry and began a poetry workshop with a few friends. They all sent their work off to magazines and saw the occasional piece in print but the next logical step was to start a magazine of their own.

Originally it was simply typed and duplicated, sold on street corners, through mail order and at poetry readings. Gradually the production became more ambitious and Ken became increasingly interested in typography and book design, wanting to produce a more professional end-product:

'In the mid 1980s, DTP started to become available. I thought that DTP skills would be useful in my job as a freelance journalist, so I borrowed £2000 and bought an Apple Mac computer and printer, together with a program called Quark Xpress. I taught myself how to use it - it was quite complicated at first but it's very easy once you get used to it. I can now produce copy that's indistinguishable from professional typesetting - because of course, that's exactly what it is!'

Ken now publishes two or three books of other people's poetry a year, under the name of Reality Studios:

'They are small editions of 300 copies each. I produce the books up to the camera ready copy stage and then

employ a printer to print and bind them. My disk can be sent straight to a typesetting machine which can output bromide or film direct from the disk.'

Ken has built up a mailing list of customers over the years and sells his books through poetry magazines and at readings and festivals:

'It is getting cheaper and easier to produce your own publications. Only a few years ago, it would have been inconceivable to be able to produce 300 copies of poetry. DTP has made it simpler and accessible to more people. There's no money in poetry publishing but it's a pleasurable pastime!'

There are a number of evening classes throughout the country where you can learn how to use DTP. Ask your local education authority for details. DTP is also an intrinsic part of many printing and publishing courses.

Printing

Book printers tend to specialise in either paperbacks or hardbacks.
Covers and jackets, although treated separately, may also be produced
at the same time.
Cox and Wyman are the UK's leading paperback printer. The chances are
that when you pick up a paperback, it will have been printed by them.
One and a half million books a week come off their presses, ready to be
distributed to the publishers' warehouses and sent to booksellers all
over the UK and Europe. 20 per cent of Cox and Wyman's production is
for publishers abroad - in fact, they print in every European language
from Icelandic to Portuguese and compete with all the European printers
for business. It takes a massive 15,000 tonnes of paper a year to feed
the hungry presses - that's five large articulated lorries' full a day. Some
of the paper is bought directly by Cox and Wyman, some supplied by
merchants and some (for all the Random House books) supplied by
Grampian Paper.
230 people work at their premises in Reading, working in shifts
to cover the 24 hour a day production necessary to compete in the
current market.

SENIOR ACCOUNT EXECUTIVE

The whole process begins in the customer service department. JANE HOLLINGS, Senior Account Executive, explains:

'I deal mainly with one very large publisher, Reed Consumer, which is split into seven imprints. I'm their contact with Cox and Wyman, so it's me they phone initially to say they want to produce a particular book. They give me the details such as page extent (how long the book is), the type of paper to be used, whether or not we will print the cover and what they will supply us with to print from.'

The print run (how many books) can be anything from 500 to over a million, but an average is around 8 - 10,000. Jane needs to know the deadline for the books to be printed - if it's a very rushed reprint, it may have to be done within a couple of days.

Cox and Wyman print text and covers and do all the foiling and embossing that you see on mass market paperbacks. The publisher sends Jane all the necessary materials, including the proposed cover. The layout for the cover is in the form of a baseboard with the lettering on, covered with tracing paper on which are written the instructions about colours to be used. If a photograph is to be included on the cover, that will come to Jane too.

A reprographic house will scan the photograph or colour artwork and 'shoot' (photograph) the baseboard, producing four films, one for each of the four printing colours used - black, magenta, yellow and cyan. Unless a special colour is mixed, these are the only four colours used in printing. Each of the colour printing units uses only one colour, printing selected areas. By the time a cover has been through all four units, the colour has built up to produce all the different colours and tones you see on any full colour picture. Sample cover sheets are sent to the publisher to be shown at sales meetings. At this stage it's not too late to make alterations.

'The Camera Ready Copy (CRC) of the text is sent to us to shoot or, if it's a reprint or there's already been a hardback, they might send us a copy of the book and we'll shoot from that. I put the text into the factory with all the details on the ticket - any reduction or enlargement in size there's to be, margins, paper to be used and the board specified for the cover. The prelims (the first few pages of a book) will probably change in paperback, so I may need to send them to be typeset, after which they'll be pasted onto board, photocopied and sent to the publisher to be proofread. Any mistakes in the hardback would also be corrected at this stage.'

Jane's role then is to keep an eye on the job as it goes through the factory. Each morning there's a meeting of all the managers and every job is discussed. Jane will chase it up if it's late, chase up the customer if they've forgotten to supply anything (such as the bar code for the cover) and answer any of the customer's queries. Once the books have been delivered, she'll send out an invoice.

It's a job which requires accuracy (mistakes in the factory can be very costly to rectify) as well as diplomacy, keeping the customer happy and liaising with the internal departments. Literacy and numeracy are essential for Jane's job ..... and to deal with overseas customers you need language skills. It's also important to be able to cope well and make decisions under pressure.

Jane took a secretarial course when she left school and worked in a variety of jobs before coming to Cox and Wyman. As well as the in-house training in each department given to every newcomer, most companies encourage further training, for instance in printing technology and business studies.

PLANNER AND PLATEMAKER

GARY CLARK is a Full Colour Planner and Platemaker, and has followed in his father's footsteps to work at Cox and Wyman:

'My dad's been here for 27 years - he came home from work one day and told me there was a job going, so I applied and got it. I started in August 1986 as an apprentice and took my City and Guilds 523 Printing and Platemaking - a two-year block release course at the London College of Printing. It teaches you all about the different methods of printing as well as full colour planning, computer studies and science.'

Gary works on the covers for paperbacks, taking the four films supplied by the reprographic house (one each for black, magenta, yellow and cyan) and mounting each on a 'carrier foil', centred on a grid. It's important that Gary's precise in his work or the finished cover will be 'out of register', with the colour not matching up properly, so he uses an eyeglass to make sure that he lines up each film exactly with the grid.

The foil is transferred to the 'step and repeat' machine which uses ultra violet (UV) light to reproduce the image from the foil onto a 'plate' and then, after Gary has turned it round, repeats it upside down so that the cover image appears twice, 'head to head' on the plate. This process is repeated so that each of the four colours has a separate plate. The four colours together will go to make up the cover. Because UV inks have been used, the plates have to be baked in an oven to harden the image onto the plate - otherwise it would start fading before all the covers had been printed.

These plates are then fixed onto cylinders, one for each colour, and the cover is printed.

Gary works a 37 and-a-half hour week, in shifts, and enjoys his job:

'Cover work's far more interesting than text. Every single job you do is different. I can walk into a bookshop and see a book and say "I've done the cover for that". It's very satisfying.'

Pre-Press Manager

Overseeing the whole of the pre-press process (before it reaches the printing presses) is **ANDREW RAE**, the Pre-Press Manager. He runs a department of 26 people who work a three-shift system, organising their rotas, making sure that jobs are going through at the right time and co-ordinating the production process with the customer services, production planning and the print room:

'We have to make sure that what we're printing on the text side is being parallelled by the cover side so that we can unite the two for binding. If necessary, we can rush a title through our process in three hours, working flat out. We delivered the reprint of John Grisham's book, *The Firm*, for instance, in two days flat - printed, bound and delivered. A publisher may ring up and say, 'I need 10,000 copies now.' We just accept all the work and juggle priorities accordingly. It's a constantly rolling process.

'It's a very varied job, combining admin' with dealing with people ..... it gets the adrenalin going!'

In the sixth form at school, Andrew took part in a project on local pubs, which was professionally typeset and printed. That's when he decided that printing looked an interesting area of work. He took a three-year HND in printing, spending the middle year out in industry, with Cox and Wyman who sponsored him through his third year. He rewarded them by winning the top prize at college and then returned to them to help set up the colour department three years ago, when his management training began.

The printing itself takes place in the print room (the factory floor). If they're printing text, each page is first photographed to produce a negative film. The pages are positioned and fixed on a 'foil' in multiples of 64 or 96 and exposed to UV light. A copy of the text appears on the light-sensitive paper underneath the foil and after it's been checked it's placed on a metal plate which is itself exposed to the UV light. The text image appears on the plate .... and it's ready to be fixed to the metal cylinders for printing. The process works by the text image picking up ink and repelling water and all other areas repelling ink and picking up water. The printed text from each plate is known as a 'working'. Workings are loaded into hoppers and collated prior to being glued together.

Like the covers, the text is printed 'head to head', so the process ends with two books still joined together in the middle. They are automatically guillotined and trimmed, packed and distributed.

The presses can deliver 40 titles a day, printing up to 20,000 workings an hour.

For more information about the printing industry including entry and training details, contact a large local printer direct or the British Printing Industries Federation.